HOW TO HELP THE PLANET

DITCHING
FOOD WASTE

by
Rebecca Phillips-Bartlett

BEARPORT
PUBLISHING

Minneapolis, Minnesota

Credits: All images are courtesy of Shutterstock.com, unless otherwise specified. With thanks to Getty Images, Thinkstock Photo, and iStockphoto. Recurring images – VectorMine, Anna Kosheleva. Cover – VectorMine, Wiro.Klyngz. 2–3 – A3pfamily. 4–5 – RaiDztor, Tatiana Gordievskaia. 6–7 – Ground Picture, Antonina Vlasova. 8–9 – Flexd Design, J.M. Image Factory. 10–11 – Jamie Rogers, Rudmer Zwerver, Timolina, neil langan, Prostock-studio, Independence_Project. 12–13 – Lamyai, chansont, DigitalPen. 14–15 – Africa Studio, Tatevosian Yana. 16–17 – Evan Lorne, aquatarkus, HollyHarry. 18–19 – Monkey Business Images, Volodymyr TVERDOKHLIB. 20–21 – Ozgur Coskun, Mehriban A. 22–23 – Rawpixel.com, Alyona Shu.

Bearport Publishing Company Product Development Team
President: Jen Jenson; Director of Product Development: Spencer Brinker; Managing Editor: Allison Juda; Associate Editor: Naomi Reich; Associate Editor: Tiana Tran; Senior Designer: Colin O'Dea; Designer: Elena Klinkner; Designer: Kayla Eggert; Product Development Assistant: Owen Hamlin

Library of Congress Cataloging-in-Publication Data is available at www.loc.gov or upon request from the publisher.

ISBN: 979-8-88916-285-8 (hardcover)
ISBN: 979-8-88916-290-2 (paperback)
ISBN: 979-8-88916-294-0 (ebook)

© 2024 BookLife Publishing
This edition is published by arrangement with BookLife Publishing.

North American adaptations © 2024 Bearport Publishing Company. All rights reserved. No part of this publication may be reproduced in whole or in part, stored in any retrieval system, or transmitted in any form or by any means, electronic, mechanical, photocopying, recording, or otherwise, without written permission from the publisher.

For more information, write to Bearport Publishing, 5357 Penn Avenue South, Minneapolis, MN 55419.

CONTENTS

Our Planet, Our Problem 4
There Is Plenty We Can Do. 6
What Is a Carbon Footprint? 8
How to Make Meat-Free Meals. . 10
How to Track Food Miles 12
How to Plan Seasonal Meals . . . 14
How to Avoid Waste 16
How to Shop for the Planet. . . . 18
How to Use Food Waste 20
We Can Help. 22
Glossary 24
Index 24

OUR PLANET, OUR PROBLEM

Earth is our home. It gives us everything we need to live. The planet takes care of us, but we are not always good at taking care of it.

Earth has been getting hotter because of things people do. This hurts the planet and all the life on it. What can we do to help?

Rising heat and other changing weather is called **climate change**.

THERE IS PLENTY WE CAN DO

Climate change is a problem, but there is plenty we can do to help the planet. Even the smallest things can make a difference.

From how we grow food to how we throw it away, small things can affect climate change. We have the power to help our planet when we choose what we put on our plate.

Food from plants is healthier for Earth and for ourselves.

WHAT IS A CARBON FOOTPRINT?

Greenhouse gases are part of what causes climate change. These gases are let out when we drive cars and make electricity.

A **carbon footprint** measures the amount of greenhouse gases a person's actions put into the air. This helps us understand how we affect the planet. The smaller our carbon footprint, the better it is for the planet!

Heating our homes creates greenhouse gases.

HOW TO MAKE MEAT-FREE MEALS

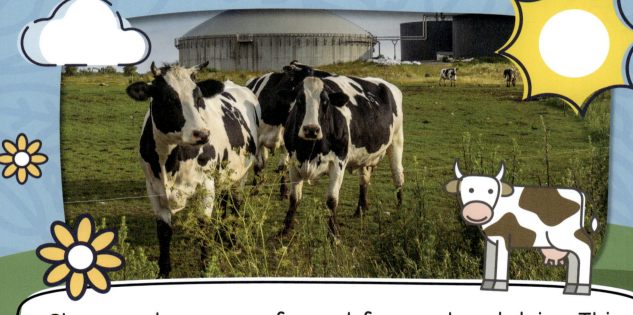

Sheep and cows are farmed for meat and dairy. This can create a lot of greenhouse gas. Eating less meat and dairy can make your carbon footprint smaller.

Try having more plant-based foods instead. Plants do not create many greenhouse gases.

Add as many fruits and vegetables to your meal as you can.

HOW TO TRACK FOOD MILES

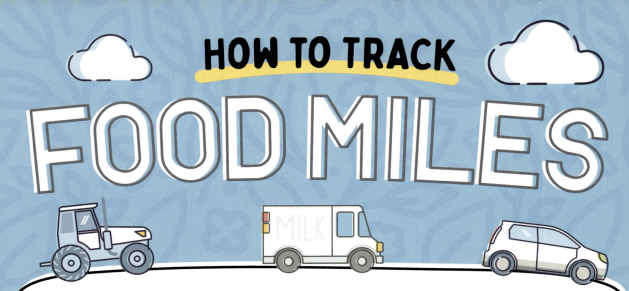

A lot of the food we eat has to travel a long way before it gets to our plates. Food miles help us measure the distance. Moving food from one place to another creates lots of greenhouse gases.

Many foods have labels on them that say where they were made or grown. We can use this to find out how far our food has traveled.

Create a meal plan to include fruits and veggies grown by farmers near you.

HOW TO PLAN SEASONAL MEALS

Each season has different foods that grow best. It takes fewer **natural resources**, such as water, to grow food that is in season.

Seasonal foods taste fresh and are full of **nutrients**.

Find out which foods are in season where you live. Make a chart that shows the best foods to eat all year long.

HOW TO AVOID WASTE

Bread is one of the most wasted foods.

Lots of food gets wasted each year. When food is left to rot rather than being eaten, it lets out greenhouse gases. Throwing away food also wastes the resources used to grow it.

Thinking ahead helps us plan how to use food so it does not go to waste. It also makes sure we buy only the food we can eat before it gets old.

HOW TO SHOP FOR THE PLANET

How we shop can help save the planet, too. A lot of food is wrapped in **plastic** that is then thrown away. This plastic stays in the environment for more than a hundred years before it breaks down.

We can help the planet by buying fewer foods wrapped this way. Shop for things that have **recyclable** packaging. Better yet, get them with no wrapping at all!

Reusable shopping bags make less trash.

HOW TO USE FOOD WASTE

ROOTS

Even when we plan meals, there are parts of some food that we cannot eat, such as the seeds and roots. But that does not mean they have to go to waste!

Start a garden in your kitchen! Try using some food scraps to grow something new. If you give some food waste water and sun, it may grow new veggies!

Some scraps of lettuce and carrots can grow into new plants.

LETTUCE

WE CAN HELP

Climate change is a big problem for our planet. However, we can make a difference with good choices about which foods we eat.

Together, we can protect the planet from climate change. Small things we do can make a big difference.

What seasonal meal will you make first?

GLOSSARY

carbon footprint a measure of the carbon dioxide and other gases released into the air because of a person's activities

climate change the change to Earth's weather patterns

greenhouse gases gases, such as carbon dioxide and methane, that trap heat around Earth

natural resources materials found in nature that people use or need

nutrients things found in food that help people or animals stay healthy

plastic a human-made material that can be shaped into almost anything

recyclable able to be made into something new

INDEX

climate change 5–8, 22–23
dairy 10
farmers 13
fruits 11, 13
greenhouse gases 8–12, 16
plastic 18
seasons 14–15, 23
shop 18–19
vegetables 11, 13
water 14, 21